No doubt you've been bombarded with "expert" advice from your parents, professors, and countless advisors. It's time you got advice you can really use—from fellow students who've been where you're headed.

All **Students Helping Students™** guides are written and edited by top students and recent grads from colleges and universities across the U.S. You'll find no preachy or condescending advice here—just stuff to help you succeed in tackling your academic, social, and professional challenges.

GETTING THE MOST
FROM STUDY ABROAD

SCORING A
GREAT INTERNSHIP

To learn more about **Students Helping Students™** guides, read samples, share your own experiences with other students, suggest a topic or ask questions, visit us at **www.studentshelpingstudents.com**!

Students Helping Students™

CONQUERING YOUR UNDERGRADUATE THESIS

First Edition

NATAVI GUIDES

New York

Conquering Your Undergraduate Thesis.
First Edition.

Published by **NATAVI GUIDES**. For information on bulk purchases or custom promotional guides, please contact the publisher via email at sales@nataviguides.com or by phone at 1.866.425.4218. You can learn more about our promotional guides program on our website, www.nataviguides.com.

Printed in the U.S.A.

ISBN 0-9719392-0-9

Library of Congress Control Number: 2002105187

Students Helping Students™
"same pager"

Before you dive into reading this guide, we'd like to share with you a bit of the philosophy on which it's based. We figure that you'll find it more useful if we're on the same page as you begin.

We think that you're pretty smart and savvy and don't like people talking down to you.

We know that you have lots to do and are interested in reading only the most relevant information.

We believe that you appreciate the value of advice given by someone who has been where you're going.

And one more thing: Don't just read this guide. <u>USE IT</u> to help you get where you're going. Write in it and on it, fold pages you find useful and refer to them later, carry it in your bag for good luck. Do whatever it is that will help you tackle the tasks before you!

the primary author

Nataly Kogan graduated from Wesleyan University in 1998. Her high honors thesis was entitled "Rule Evasion in Post-Soviet Russia." Nataly, together with her advisor, published articles based on her thesis in several academic journals and as a chapter in an anthology from Oxford University Press.

Nataly has never forgotten the feeling of her thesis carrel walls closing in on her at two in the morning, and she hopes that what she learned from the experience of working on an undergraduate thesis can help other students successfully tackle this often daunting task.

the contributors

Students from Amherst College, Columbia University, Cornell University, Hampshire College, Harvard University, Princeton University, the University of Chicago, the University of Wisconsin - Madison, Wesleyan University, and Williams College contributed to this guide.

author's note

I hope that writers of all types of theses—humanities, science, social science, creative writing—find the pieces of advice I gathered for this guide useful and helpful. My primary goal in structuring and organizing this guide was to address important questions related to the overall process of writing an undergraduate thesis. However, I feel compelled to include a disclaimer that this guide is probably most relevant for writers of social studies theses.

As you read through the guide's sections, keep in mind that the process of writing a thesis is rarely a carefully organized sequence of isolated tasks. While some steps clearly come first—choosing your topic and your advisor, for example—the others flow in and out of each other, repeat, and change in their scope and proportion. You might do some research, write part of a chapter, revise that part, find that you have to do some more research, write a bit more, and so on. Don't feel constrained by the sequence of the sections presented in this guide. Use them to help you get organized and to remember important components of each step, and adapt them to your particular thesis and working style.

Read on, write on, and remember to always think big and dream bigger.

contents

what it is

An undergraduate thesis is a research and position paper that many of us choose to write during our senior year of college. It's a really long research paper that takes one or two semesters and lots of brain cells to complete. It is the cause of much stress and anxiety, but also of the pride we feel holding the heavy bound copy of our intellectual labors once it's finished. For many of us, it's the longest piece of writing we will ever produce.

Everything you love and hate about working on a research paper is exacerbated ten-fold in a thesis. It's longer, it requires much more reflection and intricate planning, an ability to sift through ridiculous amounts of information, and perhaps, most of all, it requires that you continue to push yourself for what seems like a never-ending period of time.

However brilliant of a writer you may be, writing a killer thesis will be a challenge. A thesis requires that you not only research a particular topic in detail, but that you choose and argue a position on it, and do this through clear and cohesive writing. A thesis is called a thesis because it has one—the main argument around which you must structure your paper, and that which you must support using outside research.

Completing an undergraduate thesis can be an immensely rewarding achievement earned through hard work, guts, and persistence. Whatever your final grade might be, it will feel satisfying just to look at the side binding of your thesis and see your name on it. College is a rare time in life when you have long, uninterrupted stretches of time to think and discover and create. Completing a senior thesis is one of the best ways to take advantage of this time and to use the freshness and courage of your mind to the fullest.

what it's not

An undergraduate thesis is not the most painful and awful experience of your life. It's a challenge, but it's surmountable. You can do it.

A thesis is also not a waste of time. It might seem that way during the frequent late night when you hear a rowdy party breaking out on the lawn across from the library. You're in there slaving away and the world seems to be passing you by. Well, it's not. Working on a thesis is part of your college world, and it would be a shame to miss it. Parties happen all the time.

In a more academic light, an undergraduate thesis is not a Ph.D. dissertation or a book. It's much smaller in scope, somewhat less original, and it does not require that you study a particular topic for years before you begin to write. While some committed overachievers may aim—and succeed—in turning their theses into works worthy of dissertation status, that should not be the goal that you set out to achieve.

Finally, a thesis is not something that you HAVE to do. However rewarding and intellectually exciting it may be, working on a thesis may not be the right idea for every college student. If you picked your courses based on the fewest number of papers you'd have to write, and those you did write caused you to swear that you'd much rather visit your dentist, you should think twice about taking on a thesis.

getting organized

Forget about the fact that getting organized before you dive into your thesis will make your work better. The bigger incentive is that it will make your life easier as you work.

Even if you're someone who hates planning ahead, try to alter your usual inclinations and do it. It will greatly reduce your stress and anxiety.

START EARLY
▼
MAKE TIME
▼
DEVELOP A TIMELINE
▼
FIND GOOD WORKING SPACE

START EARLY

While you'll probably be working on your thesis during your senior year, you should begin to think about it before that year actually begins. Your school may require that you submit a thesis proposal before summer vacation, and that's a great impetus to think about your thesis early. In any case, you should start early and plan ahead.

You might want to do some background reading for your thesis, and the class-free summer months provide a perfect opportunity. As for choosing your thesis advisor, remember that professors are busy and important people—either in reality or via self-perception—and you're more likely to fare well with your advisor if you approach him or her before summer break. If you get a professor to agree to advise your thesis, he or she is likely to suggest some preliminary reading, as well. Getting these suggestions— read "requirements"—before the summer will leave you more time to follow through.

MAKE TIME

Think carefully about your class schedule during the time when you'll be working on your thesis. Senior year is a great time to have fun and take some offbeat classes outside of your major. But working on a thesis is going to require significant time and energy, so choose with care and avoid overburdening yourself.

If you're working on a two-semester thesis, try to make the second one particularly light with other coursework. Whether you're someone who plans ahead or not, the last-minute rush will catch up to you. Leave yourself time to tackle it.

"It's a great advantage to schedule classes that relate to your thesis topic. You'll find tons of relevant sources in your course syllabus, and discussing the main ideas surrounding your topic with other students and professors will force you to consider different viewpoints. You'll be working on your thesis without really having to sacrifice other course work. Also, there's a chance that you'll be able to incorporate some of your written work for your course into your thesis."

Political Science major, Princeton University '02

DEVELOP A TIMELINE

Make a rough calendar of your thesis process before you dive into it. When do you think you'll need to complete most of your research? When do you need to have your first draft finished?

To help you, consider a few deadlines that are set in stone. One is obvious: The day when your thesis is due. There are probably a few others that vary by school, which might include a mid-point check-in with your department, or a certain number of chapters to be submitted to your advisor. Write these dates on paper and plan your work around them. Your timeline will certainly change many times, but by doing this you'll have a baseline from which you can change.

Feeling organized gets you well on your way to being organized.

FIND GOOD WORKING SPACE

If you're lucky, your school provides thesis carrels to thesis writers. However big or small, having a place dedicated to your thesis is extremely useful. You're going to accumulate dozens of books, notebooks, magazines, snacks, and various other things as you work, and if you can store them all in one place, your life will be easier.

If you don't have a thesis carrel, really think about where you'll be doing most of your reading, thinking, and writing. Libraries, reading rooms, and your room are all good choices, but how good they are will vary based on your particular set-up. Give this some thought. Having a dedicated thesis space that is free of rowdy roommates and is off the path frequented by drunken party crowds will help you focus and get your work done much better and faster, and it will get you on your way to joining the party crowd, or doing whatever else you enjoy.

choosing your topic

Choosing an interesting and appropriate topic for your thesis is more important and challenging than it might initially seem. You probably know the general subject area where your thesis will originate. Most likely, this area is your major, but you might choose to write an interdisciplinary thesis or focus on a completely different academic discipline. Figuring out the general subject area of your thesis is the first and easiest step. The next general step is to figure out what your particular topic will be, and finally, what thesis—position or argument—about that topic you'll present in your work.

Below are some suggestions for what to consider as you think about your thesis topic.

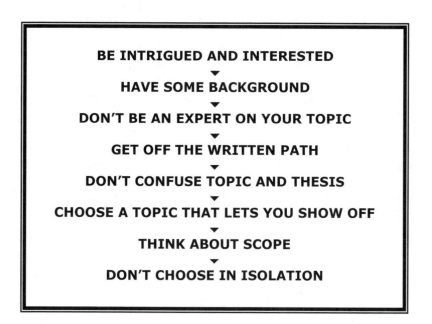

BE INTRIGUED AND INTERESTED
▼
HAVE SOME BACKGROUND
▼
DON'T BE AN EXPERT ON YOUR TOPIC
▼
GET OFF THE WRITTEN PATH
▼
DON'T CONFUSE TOPIC AND THESIS
▼
CHOOSE A TOPIC THAT LETS YOU SHOW OFF
▼
THINK ABOUT SCOPE
▼
DON'T CHOOSE IN ISOLATION

BE INTRIGUED AND INTERESTED

For many months, your thesis will occupy a disproportionately large amount of your thoughts. You'll be much happier if you're constantly thinking about something that is interesting and intriguing to you. Being interested in your topic will also improve the quality of your work. The last thing you need is to be bored by your thesis.

This is a somewhat intuitive point, but really do consider it seriously. It's not difficult to be influenced by a professor or someone else and choose a topic that interests them. But that professor is not the one who is going to be writing dozens of pages on this topic and thinking about it day and night. You are. Figure out what genuinely interests you and don't shy away because of someone else's reaction. Suggestions from trusted professors, parents, and friends are great as things to think about, and you shouldn't brush them aside. But you know best what intrigues you, and you should try to write your thesis about something that does.

"I didn't realize how easy it would be to get bored with my subject matter. When I started, I was thrilled. I thought I had chosen a topic near and dear to my heart. But, after a few late nights and some bad data, the whole process just wasn't fun anymore."

**Economics major,
Harvard University '98**

A NOTE ON INTEREST VS. PASSION

Being interested in something does not mean being passionate about it. If you're a political science major and are also a passionate and devoted Democrat, writing about the history of the Democratic Party in the U.S. may not necessarily be your best bet. Your passions may sway you away from careful research and thought, and they may limit your readiness to understand and write about all the relevant sides of your argument. This may not happen, but if you're thinking about writing your thesis on a topic that is very dear to your heart and mind, consider the possible consequences and what you might need to do in order to mitigate them.

HAVE SOME BACKGROUND

A senior thesis is an advanced project. It leaves little room for basic research and discovery on a topic about which you know absolutely nothing. One or two semesters may seem like a long period of time, but it's not enough time to learn about something on both a basic and a very detailed level, and then write a long paper intelligently formulating and arguing a strong thesis.

While you should have some general understanding of your topic, you don't need to have specific and detailed knowledge about it. The main purpose behind writing a thesis is to research a general topic, find a specific area within it on which you want to focus, and then formulate and argue a thesis about that area.

Here's an example. Not knowing anything about Latin American economies is a general issue. Not knowing the details behind Argentina's debt default is a specific issue that might actually make a great thesis topic for someone who has some background in economics and Latin America.

DON'T BE AN EXPERT ON YOUR TOPIC

Having several months to learn about something in extreme detail is a precious opportunity you'll rarely have after college. It would be a shame if you gave it up by writing your thesis on a topic in which you're an expert.

True, the end product may be stellar, but you'll miss out on a chance to learn something new, and to learn it well.

> "Probably the most rewarding part of working on my thesis was the chance to become an expert on a particular topic."

**English major,
Wesleyan University '99**

GET OFF THE WRITTEN PATH

If the library shelves are filled with books covering the potential subject of your thesis through ten different angles, maybe you should reconsider. Not that you couldn't come up with a brilliant thesis that presents the topic through an eleventh angle, but your chances of finding and presenting a strong and innovative argument are greater if you choose something about which hundreds of other academics have not written.

> "Frankly, at least in history, the greatest challenge is being able to say something original about your topic, to not just do a book report on the literature in your research. You need to find a niche for yourself in a pre-existing field and aim to write something that contributes to that field."

**History major,
Wesleyan University '99**

Once you have a few ideas for a topic, go to the library and check out a few sources for each. Read through their introductions and a few paragraphs—this will give you an idea of how much has been written on your particular topic and whether you want to choose a different one.

A NOTE ON INNOVATION

While we often tend to think of innovation in terms of ground-breaking inventions, that's just one kind, and one that is extremely rare. Most innovations in the world, and in academia in particular, are much more incremental and less earth shattering. To borrow a bit from Thomas Kuhn, most innovations are not paradigm shifts, but rather, shifts within a certain paradigm.

In other words, while your thesis and its central argument should be innovative, this does not mean that it has to argue something that has never been argued before. This is possible, but not always achievable. What your thesis should most definitely do is present a topic or a specific argument about that topic in a different light than what has been done previously.

After reading your work, an expert in that particular field should feel that your thesis somehow has contributed to the overall debate about the topic. In some cases, this might mean that you presented an argument on a particular issue not previously explored in depth. In others, it might be that you summarized and synthesized the existing debate on a topic in a unique way that has not been done before.

DON'T CONFUSE TOPIC AND THESIS

The reason this very long senior-year paper is called a thesis is because it has one. A thesis is an argument, a point of view about a certain subject, event, relationship, etc. And the entire purpose of working on a thesis is to research and present this argument as completely and persuasively as possible.

Choosing a topic for your thesis is very different from deciding what your argument—your thesis—will be about this topic. While you might have a general idea of what your argument might be, it's likely that it will change and get more precise as you research and write (more on that in later chapters). In fact, a significant portion of the time you spend on your thesis will be spent figuring out precisely what your central argument should be.

Your topic should be general enough to allow you room to find things to argue about it. If you start off too narrow, you run the risk of not having enough to write about.

CHOOSE A TOPIC THAT LETS YOU SHOW OFF

You've learned a thing or two in college. And you've even learned a few things that are academically inclined. There's no better place to show off your skills than in your undergraduate thesis. Not just for the benefit of your advisor, professors, and proud parents, but for your own wonderful and bright self.

When thinking about your thesis topic, consider whether it is broad and complex enough to allow your skills to shine. If you're an interdisciplinary major, for example, maybe you should select a topic that allows you to apply analytical frameworks from more than one discipline. If you speak a foreign language or have studied one while in college, you might want to choose a topic that involves foreign language research. Think about what particular or unique skills you've gained during the past few years and how you might show them off in your thesis.

THINK ABOUT SCOPE

Whatever topic you choose to write about, make sure that its scope allows you to research and write a well-argued and complete paper. No, it does not have to be a book or a Master's dissertation, but your thesis should be compelling, and to be compelling, it has to be thorough. Think about the scope of your topic and whether you can adequately explore and write about it in one or two semesters. Arguing a particular view on the history of the world might not be your best bet for a thesis.

DON'T CHOOSE IN ISOLATION

You are the final judge of what you want and can write about in your thesis. But it's a good idea to talk about your ideas with a professor or two before you commit. The professor does not have to be your advisor, but he or she should be someone who has knowledge of the subject area you're considering and whose opinion you trust. Professors have seen hundreds of students succeed and fail at writing theses, and they will definitely have some ideas for you.

"Contacting professors, graduate students, and even other undergrads before you start is a great way to get some ideas about your topic. People can often be better resources than books when you begin thinking about your topic because they challenge you to express your own ideas clearly."

**Political Science major,
Princeton University '02**

topic notes

_____

_____

_____

_____

_____

_____

_____

_____

_____

_____

_____

_____

_____

_____

finding a great advisor

Finding the right advisor to guide you along your thesis path is really important. It's perhaps more important than many of us initially realize, and too many aspiring thesis writers have suffered because they made their choice without thinking too much about it.

A good advisor will read your work, make comments and suggestions, alert you to sources that you might not have considered, and share his/her insights with you. A great advisor will become your thought partner, working through your arguments, challenging your assumptions, and opening up new ways to consider common issues. He or she will become personally invested both in your work and in its success.

Put some effort into finding the right advisor and remember not to wait until the last minute.

LOOK FOR EXPERIENCE AND EXPERTISE
▼
FIND AN ADVISOR WANTING TO ADVISE
▼
LOOK FOR A PERSONALITY MATCH
▼
ASK AROUND
▼
SELL YOURSELF AND YOUR THESIS

LOOK FOR EXPERIENCE AND EXPERTISE

Your advisor will be of little help to you unless he or she is familiar with the general topic of your thesis and is expert in the academic discipline from which it stems. If you're thinking of writing about French intellectual history, your advisor might be from the history or philosophy department, and should have some familiarity with French intellectuals.

Although you probably know the professors in your academic discipline quite well, do some checking. What have they written? What courses have they taught? You should get some pretty strong clues as to whether your topic and your advisor are a good fit.

FIND AN ADVISOR WANTING TO ADVISE

Advising a thesis is not as demanding as writing one, but it does add to a professor's workload and responsibility. Your advisor should understand this and should want to do it. It's a good idea to have a casual conversation with your potential advisor about his or her schedule for the year, availability, and ability to devote time to working with you.

Don't take it personally if a professor refuses to be your advisor. Many are too busy, and some say no because they don't feel that they can contribute to your particular topic. You're better off knowing this before you start.

Your advisor should also be interested in what you're writing about. Interest invokes thought, and thought and inquisitive questions are something you very much want your advisor to have about your thesis. When you speak to a professor about your thesis ideas, pay attention to his or her level of interest and factor this into your decision.

LOOK FOR A PERSONALITY MATCH

A relationship between you and your advisor is different than one between you and a class professor. You'll work together more often and more closely, and you'll work one-on-one most of the time. If you bond with your advisor on a personal level, it's a great bonus, but it's not something that is critical to the success of your thesis.

Make sure that you work well with your advisor and that your working styles mesh well together. If you're someone who needs an occasional push or deadline enforcement, then your advisor should be someone who is willing to push. If you need encouragement, then your advisor should be someone open to providing it.

The bottom line is that you should feel comfortable working and talking with your advisor. He or she shouldn't make you feel nervous or intimidated or discouraged. You aren't likely to gain much from your advisor's words of wisdom if you cringe at the mere sound of his or her voice.

ASK AROUND

Talk to the professors in the department where you're searching for an advisor. Do they know who might be interested? Who might be the expert on your topic? Who is taking on thesis students next year?

Once you have an idea who you might like to have as your advisor, talk to professors and students about him or her. Do they think the two of you are a good match? What is the professor like in class and during office hours? You can learn a lot about someone from his or her colleagues and students, so do your homework.

Really great resources, if you can get in touch with them, are students your potential advisor has advised in the past. They can tell you better than anyone what it's like to work with a particular professor, so try and seek them out. An email is a simple and non-intrusive way to ask a few questions. Keep in mind, however, that relationships are subjective, so always take what you hear with a serious grain of salt.

SELL YOURSELF AND YOUR THESIS

Choosing your advisor is step one. Getting your advisor to choose you is step two, and you might have to work for this one as well. Remember that you're not the only one looking for an advisor.

When approaching a professor, have a good idea of the general topic of your thesis. Tell him or her about it, why you think it is interesting and fresh and new, and most importantly, why you think it matches the professor's interests and area of expertise.

"You can really hook an advisor if you show off your zeal and commitment to the topic, and the thesis process in general."

**History major,
Wesleyan University '99**

Don't forget to also sell yourself a bit. Talk about your experience on the topic, why you're interested in writing about it, and how hard you'll work to make your thesis a strong one. Professors love having advisees who receive honors (or a similar high grade), and it's a plus for their career and their reputation.

Timing is key here, as well. The earlier you approach a potential advisor, the more likely you are to be the first one to do so. Being first does not make it a done deal, but it does allow you to talk to someone who is not yet inundated with requests. It also shows that you plan ahead and are serious about your thesis—two things all advisors like to see.

working with your advisor

Your advisor can either be a great asset, a neutral observer, or an obstacle to be overcome on your way to thesis success. What your particular situation will be depends on many factors, such as your advisor's personality, your personality, the way you work together, the type of relationship that you form, and many, many more. Some of these are just human nature and there isn't much you can do to change them. Just try to deal the best way you can.

There are some factors, however, that you can control to make sure that your working relationship with your advisor is effective and helpful to your progress. Here are a few of them.

SET EXPECTATIONS UPFRONT
▼
BE PROACTIVE
▼
BE HONEST
▼
PREPARE FOR MEETINGS
▼
SAY THANK YOU

SET EXPECTATIONS UPFRONT

Communication is a good thing. Use it. Talk to your advisor early on about how the two of you will work together. Will you have weekly status meetings to discuss where you are and where you might need to be headed in your writing or research? We highly recommend that you do in fact establish a meeting schedule. But the most important thing is that you and your advisor both know and expect the same—a regularly scheduled meeting if you agreed to it, or a meeting by appointment, if that's what you decided.

Talk about how involved you'd like your advisor to be in your research and your work. Will he or she be reading drafts often? Or are you going to agree on a few times during the year when you'll give your advisor certain chapters on which to comment?

Make sure you know what your advisor prefers in terms of communication between your meetings. Is phone or email better? When is the best time to call? What are your advisor's busiest days when it might not be a good idea to show up at his or her door?

While not everything you might talk about at the beginning will stay consistent throughout, it will get the two of you started on great terms. By showing your advisor that the way you two communicate and the way you receive his or her feedback is important to you, you're showing that you're respectful of their time. Busy professors like to be respected.

BE PROACTIVE

If you want your advisor to recommend a source, ask. If you'd like him or her to read a draft of one of your chapters, ask. If you had a meeting planned and your advisor didn't show up, ask why not.

Be proactive and straightforward. Your advisor is not doing you a favor by being your advisor. He or she has agreed to do it and, as a result, has assumed certain responsibilities. This doesn't mean, however, that your advisor will be proactive with following through on these responsibilities.

That's your job, so don't be shy.

BE HONEST

"Be honest with your advisor about everything. They are there to give advice, to coach you, support you as well as grade you. If you aren't honest with them about the troubles you are having—with procrastination, writing, or anything—how are they supposed to help you? Meet with them often, it will help you stay motivated and focused. Advisors are an excellent resource—for books, inspiration, contacts, and editing. Use them."

**Theater and Psychology major,
Hampshire College '02**

There is a chance that your advisor is not someone you'll know well before you two start working together. You may not know his or her quirks and ways of communication very well. And there may come a day when you ask for your advisor's feedback on your work and you can't tell what he or she really thinks. Be honest in admitting this and ask for clarification.

Being honest with your advisor will improve the quality of your thesis and will gain you respect. As students, we don't generally like feeling ambiguous about our academic performance. Don't create unnecessary stress for yourself during this already stressful time.

author's corner
▼

My advisor was a perfectly nice man and we got along wonderfully. But any time I'd ask him what he thought about my thesis, he'd say something so cryptic and ambiguous that I never knew what he really thought of it. "It's judicious," he wrote on one of my mid-semester evaluations.

I never pressed him for a better answer and spent the year in ambiguity stress. "He's British," I'd console myself, "he can't express praise as unabashedly as we Americans do."

Maybe so, but I wish I'd given him a chance to try by pressing him to really tell me what he thought during the seven months before he gave my thesis a stellar final evaluation.

▲

PREPARE FOR MEETINGS

"Make sure to prepare carefully before going to meet your advisor to make sure you use the time efficiently. "

**Economics major,
Harvard University '98**

It's great if you have a rapport with your advisor and can talk without end during meetings. But chatting for an hour about last night's game or sharing department gossip is not going to help your thesis. For your advisor to help you with, and contribute to, your thesis, your meetings need to be constructive. It's your responsibility to make them that way.

Think about the few key questions or issues that you need to discuss prior to the meeting, and tell your advisor upfront what they are. If you have questions about a certain source, bring the source with you. If you'd like your advisor to read a short piece of your thesis, make sure to bring an extra copy.

SAY THANK YOU

Thank your advisor often and as genuinely as you can. This is a good rule in life in general, but doing so can create lots of good vibes during your thesis process. And don't forget to include your advisor in your Acknowledgements.

advisor notes

_____

_____

_____

_____

_____

_____

_____

_____

_____

_____

_____

_____

_____

_____

_____

researching your thesis

Well, here it goes. The real deal. You've organized your time and space, chosen an intriguing topic, and found a wonderful advisor. If it were only that easy.

Your research skills are one of the two main components that your thesis is meant to test—your ability to construct and write clear arguments being the other. Before you type any words related to your topic into a library database or an Internet search engine—and then lose your eyeballs as they jump from their sockets—read through the suggestions below. The amount of information on most every topic is vast and daunting, so approaching it with a specific strategy in mind is in your best interest.

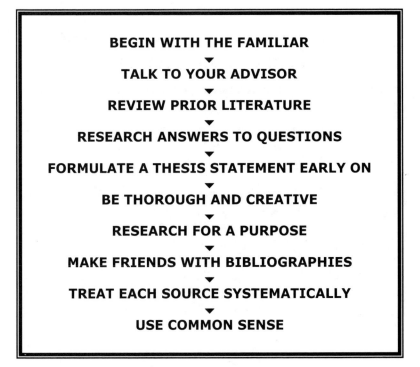

BEGIN WITH THE FAMILIAR
▼
TALK TO YOUR ADVISOR
▼
REVIEW PRIOR LITERATURE
▼
RESEARCH ANSWERS TO QUESTIONS
▼
FORMULATE A THESIS STATEMENT EARLY ON
▼
BE THOROUGH AND CREATIVE
▼
RESEARCH FOR A PURPOSE
▼
MAKE FRIENDS WITH BIBLIOGRAPHIES
▼
TREAT EACH SOURCE SYSTEMATICALLY
▼
USE COMMON SENSE

BEGIN WITH THE FAMILIAR

If you can start somewhere you've been before, you'll ease yourself into the research and avoid initial shocks. Perhaps you wrote a paper on a subject similar to your thesis topic. Or maybe there was a book you read when thinking about your topic that was helpful.

Go back to the beginning and re-read these familiar sources. It will get your mind thinking about your topic, but more importantly, these sources will likely have a bibliography that can be your initial guide to researching your thesis.

TALK TO YOUR ADVISOR

After you've put all that effort into getting the perfect advisor, it would be a shame to underutilize this resource as you plan out your initial research.

It's not a great idea to just show up at your advisor's office and say: "Hi, I'm starting to work on my thesis, what do you think I should read first?" A better approach is to say something like: "I'm beginning to work on my research and here are a few books/articles I'm planning to read first. Do you think this makes sense? Do you have any suggestions of sources that might be useful?" In other words, suggest something first, then ask for feedback. By doing this, you're not looking for an easy way out of doing the thinking yourself and you're showing that you have respect for the professor's knowledge on the subject.

REVIEW PRIOR LITERATURE

Although your experience may vary based on your academic discipline, you'll need to do a literature review at the beginning of your research. "Literature review'" is just a fancy term for becoming familiar with the existing literature—books, articles, papers—on your particular topic.

As a scholar, you are part of a broader community of academics who have thought and written about your topic. Your thesis, therefore, is not an independently standing piece of work, but rather, it's part of a wider body of knowledge and ideas in your discipline. By conducting a thorough literature review at the beginning of your research, you're making that connection between what has been studied and said before you and what your thesis is about to contribute. In many cases, the first part of your thesis will consist of summarizing your literature review and then outlining how your work will contribute to the knowledge on the subject.

This part of your research can seem quite dull and overwhelming, especially if you've chosen a popular topic. You might be discouraged and feel like you're regurgitating information. But this step is important, and it should provide you with insight on what position you might assume, and how it's unique and valid.

RESEARCH ANSWERS TO QUESTIONS

You're less likely to get lost in the quagmire of your college library if the purpose of your research is to answer questions that you pose to yourself. There are general questions that relate to your topic, and then there are more specific ones. Common sense suggests that you start with the former, and then carefully and thoughtfully progress to the latter. In fact, when you begin your thesis—and if you've followed some of our suggestions for choosing your topic—you shouldn't be able to pose extremely specific questions about it. You simply don't know enough yet to do that, and that's the idea behind research.

So, what are some general questions you could ask about your topic? How about the theoretical frameworks that are commonly used to discuss it? Or, perhaps you need to read up on the historical period most relevant to your topic? Ask yourself what you absolutely must understand and know about your topic to come up with a compelling thesis, and then go and find answers through your research.

The more you learn about your topic and the arguments that will support your thesis statement, the more specific your questions will get. Your research will get both easier and tougher as this happens. Easier because you will have a good base of knowledge and will not feel overwhelmed. Tougher because finding answers to more specific questions will require greater creativity and perseverance. Push on, though, and think about how much you're learning.

FORMULATE A THESIS STATEMENT EARLY ON

Your thesis statement will change many times throughout the process. It will likely start off very broad and general, and as you learn more, it will get more targeted and specific. This is fine, and this is the way good theses get developed.

What's important is that you're always thinking about what your thesis is and what arguments and evidence you'll need to find in order to support it. After you've done a bit of research, write down a few ideas of what your thesis statement might be. What point do you think you want to argue? What are some preliminary ideas for how you will do this? What are your main supporting arguments?

A good thesis statement is neither simple, nor straightforward. Its main argument is specific enough to be presented and supported in about a hundred pages, but complex enough that the reader will actually need to read those hundred pages to understand it. A good thesis statement is more than your opinion on the topic. It is your position on the topic supported by strong arguments and evidence.

Force yourself to develop a preliminary thesis statement early on, well before you complete most of your research. Always come back to it after you read a few sources, reevaluate and rework it. Your thesis will only benefit.

author's corner
▼
I started my thesis-filled senior year by writing down a short thesis statement with a thick black marker:

The Mafia destroyed Russia.

Four months, dozens of books, and hundreds of articles later, and too-many-to-count talks with my advisor, I crossed it out and replaced it with a new one:

The Mafia might have saved Russia from complete collapse.

It was scary to change direction like that so far into the thesis process, but I'm glad that I did it. It turned out to be a somewhat controversial point that apparently not many others had argued previously.

▲

SAMPLE TEMPLATE

Here's a template that you can use to help you think about your thesis statement and supporting arguments. Adapt it to your particular thesis and use it to help you focus your research and writing.

Overall Topic	
Thesis Statement	
Supporting Argument #1	
Supporting Argument #2	
Supporting Argument #3	

BE THOROUGH AND CREATIVE

The literature review you complete at the outset of your thesis is just the beginning—the foundation for what you'll need to research and understand as you get more and more detailed in your questions. As you progress down the research path, be creative in the ways you find useful and unique information. Part of what an undergraduate thesis tests, in fact, is your ability to find important and relevant sources, read through them, and pick out the critical information that is necessary to make your thesis cohesive and powerful.

Depending on the size and resources of your school, as well as your topic, the library will have many of the research materials you'll need. Don't be shy about talking with the librarians as they know quite a bit and may have some useful suggestions.

The Internet has come a long way in allowing us to access materials that may be in a library thousands of miles away. But be smart about how you spend your time online, as it can really suck you in. See if you can find organizations that might be related to your topic and scour their discussions, reading lists, reports, and other data. Many conferences now post their discussions and presentations online as well. Find those that are related to your topic and get a hold of the materials.

Remember also that the sources you'll be using won't always be in print form. There may have been a great documentary film on the topic, a radio show, or a symposium. Don't overlook these.

Try and maintain a constant dialogue with your advisor about where you're headed with your research, and ask for suggestions. Don't wait, ask. But always remember to outline your own plan first.

Finally, there are a few newly emerged resources that allow you to search thousands of pages of books online. Check out the "**helpful resources**" section for some ideas.

"Read everything. Consider everything. Don't ignore any lead or possibility."

**History major,
University of Wisconsin '99**

A NOTE ON PRIMARY VS. SECONDARY SOURCES

You might remember this from high school, but it can't hurt to review this very important distinction. Primary sources are those created and left behind by the participants of historical events, such as letters, diaries, manuscripts, and newspaper articles written at the time of these events. Primary sources allow you, the researcher, to get as close to these historical events as possible, and to formulate your own conclusions about them.

Secondary sources are interpretations of primary sources created after certain events took place. A history textbook is a great example of a secondary source.

As you research, you should aim to locate as many primary sources related to your topic and thesis as possible. By reading through them, you'll be able to formulate your own analysis of particular issues and events, and your chances of writing an original thesis will be greatly improved. Depending on your topic, primary sources may be plentiful or scarce, but you should do the legwork necessary to find them.

Milk secondary sources for what they're worth—great syntheses of information, summaries of analyses, and opinions on particular topics. Your literature review, for example, will consist largely of reading through secondary sources.

RESEARCH FOR A PURPOSE

If you chose well, you've selected a thesis topic that interests you. You can't wait to read the many great sources that you've managed to dig up. And, as you find yourself sitting in a comfy armchair in the library on a rainy Sunday afternoon reading one of these great sources, you might feel quite happy to be working on your thesis after all.

And you should be. But what you should not forget is that there is a purpose to what you're doing and to what you're reading. And that purpose stretches beyond enriching your mind. The reason you're reading through the sources is to learn important and relevant information for your thesis, to understand the ideas and their relationship to your own arguments, and to find evidence that either supports or weakens your thesis. To do this well, you must maintain an analytical mindset as you research. You have to consistently ask yourself why the source and the ideas you're reading are important, how they're relevant, where in your thesis you may need to refer to them, and in what context.

Enjoy your thesis research, learn new ideas, and be inspired. But don't lose your analytical edge. Don't forget to constantly think, think, think about why what you're reading is important, and how it can enrich your thesis.

MAKE FRIENDS WITH BIBLIOGRAPHIES

Reading footnotes and bibliographies is not something that many of us do, or like to do. But as you research your thesis, these resources will prove to be invaluable fountains of information, most importantly by suggesting what other research materials you might need to consider.

If you have to choose the lesser of two evils, go for bibliographies. Look for books and articles that might be relevant to your topic. Also, look for authors who seem to be experts in a related field and then check whether they have written anything else that might be helpful.

This is a tedious part of your research, but it will pay off. Try to be disciplined about it.

TREAT EACH SOURCE SYSTEMATICALLY

Chances are that you're not going to have enough time, patience, or interest to read through each of your sources in detail. And you shouldn't. Your thesis will get no better if you read a thousand pages. It will only get better if you read pages with important, interesting, and relevant information that furthers the depth and strength of your thesis.

With this in mind, there will be many sources from which you read just a few pages, or even just a paragraph. As you move deeper into your thesis, the questions that you research will get much more specific, and you'll have to become more inventive in looking for information. To make sure that you can find the critical information without wasting time, develop a system for how you'll work with each source.

Here's one example of how you might want to do this:

- Check the table of contents to find the most relevant sections.
- Skim through the introduction. This is usually the roadmap to the book or article, and it will help you focus on the source's key sections.
- After you find relevant chapters or sections, read them and take notes. Write down enough information so that it will make sense to you when you read it months later, but avoid taking down sentences word for word.
- Make sure that you indicate from which source the information is coming. It's also useful to write a note to yourself about where in your thesis you think this information may be relevant.
- For each section that you read, it will be useful to write down a few words to capture the main idea or argument that you might use in your thesis.
- Check out the footnotes in the relevant sections and the bibliography as discussed earlier.

Use this brief outline as your guide, or develop your own system. But do develop one because it will end up saving you days.

A NOTE ON KEEPING TRACK OF YOUR RESEARCH

It's impossible to say this too much: Create a clear and simple system for keeping track of all of your research and use it. Some people like note cards, some prefer notebooks—it makes no difference. Choose a method that you like best and stick with it. Write down every source, its title, author, date of publication, and what about the source is relevant to your thesis.

Also, write down where the source is from and where it is located—library, your room, your parents' house, etc. Invariably, there will come one day when you spend hours looking for that article you absolutely must re-read. Having a good system to keep track of all of your research will help minimize the number of hours you spend looking for it.

USE COMMON SENSE

Not all books and articles are valuable, many are not very original, and most are biased towards a certain belief or argument. The fact that a certain idea appears in a book does not make it an absolute truth—even if it is presented as such.

As you approach each source, take a moment to familiarize yourself with the writer, the writer's background and academic discipline. (Economists and historians can approach the same concept in two very different ways, for example.) Keep this information fresh in your mind as you read.

When you find arguments and ideas to which you may want to refer in your thesis, look for what type of evidence the author is using to support them. Ask yourself whether the author is stating his or her opinion or whether the author is presenting an argument supported by evidence.

Maintain a critical eye and you won't fall prey to using arguments that are unsubstantiated and weak. If an idea appeals to you, but is not well supported in this particular source, find another source with a more persuasive argument. You don't want someone else's flaw to taint your own work.

researching notes

_____

_____

_____

_____

_____

_____

_____

_____

_____

_____

_____

_____

_____

_____

writing your thesis

However great a writer you might be, writing your thesis will be a challenge. There aren't many students who aren't at least somewhat intimidated by the task, and those who claim that they aren't are definitely covering up. Take a deep breath and try to think about how much you're learning. If that fails to encourage you, imagine that in several months this will all be behind you and you'll be thesis-free forever. This one usually works.

Before we dive into our suggestions for how to put your thoughts, arguments, and twenty pads of notes from your research on paper—a quick note about our approach.

This guide is not here to tell you how to write a paper. If you're reading this, you have successfully made it through a few years of college and have written more than a few papers. You're an expert.

With that in mind, we've gathered a few things to look out for, suggestions for how to approach the overall writing process, and ideas to help you get on your way. We'd rather not claim expertise where others are more qualified, and if you do have more technical questions—say, how to properly format footnotes—there are some great resources to check out. (We've listed some in the "**helpful resources**" section for you.)

BEGIN TO WRITE EARLY
▼
START WITH ANYTHING BUT THE INTRO
▼
DON'T OUTLINE EVERY PARAGRAPH
▼
MAKE EACH CHAPTER STAND ON ITS OWN
▼
DON'T WRITE A CHAPTER FOR A CHAPTER'S SAKE
▼
BE WILLING TO REWRITE
▼
THINK ABOUT YOUR READER
▼
AVOID USING A STIFF AND FORMAL TONE
▼
DON'T OVERUSE EVIDENCE TO IMPRESS
▼
GIVE CREDIT GENEROUSLY
▼
MAKE YOUR CONCLUSION MORE THAN A
SUMMARY

BEGIN TO WRITE EARLY

"I wrote my thesis over spring break. Don't do that."

**Anthropology major,
University of Chicago '99**

Whatever you do, don't wait until you've finished all of your research to begin writing. Don't even wait until you have finished a big chunk of it. Our brains can't hold an unlimited amount of information, and you'll begin to forget important points and details from your first source by the time you read your twentieth. And even if you take notes while you read, looking at your notes two months after you wrote them isn't likely to fully refresh your mind.

"It's good to have a lot of sources, but you need to know when to stop researching and start writing. If you think you are procrastinating the writing and doing way too much research, you probably need to start writing. Sources are good, but so is your own voice, don't forget to use it and respect it."

**Theater and Psychology major,
Hampshire College '02**

Begin to write early, after you've read a few sources and formulated your initial thesis statement. Don't worry at that point about style, organization, or details. Just get some words and sentences and paragraphs on paper and you'll be amazed at how much easier the writing process will become. Writing down your ideas and arguments will clarify them and expose areas you might need to research further. You'll be able to see if your argument flows together or if you're forcing it along. (At which point you'll need to think it through and figure out if you're headed in the right direction and if you need further evidence to support your points.)

Most importantly, getting words on paper will help you feel less intimidated by the prospect of writing dozens or hundreds of pages. The blinking curser at the top of an empty computer screen never made anyone feel good or confident. By beginning to write early, you will avoid this ghastly image, and you'll feel more in control of the vast body of research material you've amassed.

As you begin to write, be cognizant of the fact that you are writing in semi-darkness. You haven't yet figured out all of the arguments, ideas, facts, and details that will eventually fill your thesis and your initial paragraphs will probably be very general. As you research more, you'll need to go back to these initial pages and revise them. But you'll already have something to start with, rather than a blank page and a nervous bug in your stomach.

> *"My biggest challenge was getting started. I locked myself in my room until I got going."*
>
> **History major,**
> **University of Wisconsin '99**

START WITH ANYTHING BUT THE INTRO

You've probably heard this before: Don't let the introduction be the first part of your thesis that you write.

The purpose of the introduction is to outline for your reader the main issues and arguments that you'll cover in your thesis and to broadly indicate the order in which you'll present them. After reading your introduction, the reader should have a clear idea about your thesis statement and what types of arguments you'll be discussing to support it. When you begin to write your thesis, you won't yet have a clear idea of these concepts, so you're better off waiting until later to write the introduction.

There aren't too many of us who are comfortable writing out of order. Try to overcome this barrier and skip writing the introduction until you've at least written your first chapter. Or, write a really short intro to get yourself going, but don't labor over it for too long. You'll appreciate how much easier it will be to write a grand introduction once all the arguments and ideas in your thesis are clear in your mind.

DON'T OUTLINE EVERY PARAGRAPH

Remember when we were learning how to write research papers in high school and our English teachers asked us to make an outline full of Roman numerals, quotes, and references back to the original source? Well, some things are better left in the past. If you attempt to put together an extremely detailed outline for your entire thesis, you'll go nuts. Guaranteed. This doesn't mean that you won't be able to do it. But without a doubt, you'll drive yourself crazy and, more importantly, you'll likely spend time writing something in an outline that you're better off writing in your thesis itself.

A better idea is to compose a general and brief outline of the overall structure of your thesis, its chapters, and its core points—a bird's eye roadmap that you can hang on the wall next to your computer, and which will show you where you've been and where you should be headed. A helpful outline will list the main ideas and arguments for each chapter, the primary research resources that you'll need to use to develop your line of thought, and a few specific points that you want to make sure to include. Think of this outline as a brief conversation you're having with someone about your thesis.

"So, tell me what you're writing about in your thesis?" says your imaginary inquirer.

"Well, my thesis is about the reasons behind Pepsi's dominance of the Eastern European market for the past thirty years. My main argument is that Pepsi is so ever-present because it's less fizzy than Coke and research has shown that Eastern Europeans dislike overly fizzy drinks. A great deal has been written about this subject, and I summarize the arguments to date in my first chapter. In my second and third I am going to explore the origins of low-fizz preference by the Eastern Europeans and the marketing genius of Pepsi for recognizing this quality. My fourth and final chapter discusses the future of Pepsi's dominance in Eastern Europe and considers whether Coke or any other competitor has a chance to gain market share."

There it is, the initial outline of your thesis. Break it up, add sources and key details here and there, and you have it. As you write, you can refer to it, make changes, and add sources and details. An outline is meant to help you, not overwhelm or confuse you.

SAMPLE OUTLINE TEMPLATE

Here's a simple template that you can use to begin to outline the main structure of your thesis. Feel free to copy it and fill in the appropriate sections as they relate to your thesis.

Thesis Statement

Chapter One

1. Main argument
2. Main supporting points
   a.
   b.
   c.
3. Key sources
4. Key data, quotes, statistics

Chapter Two

1. Main argument
2. Main supporting points
   a.
   b.
   c.
3. Key sources
4. Key data, quotes, statistics

Repeat for additional chapters in your thesis.

MAKE EACH CHAPTER STAND ON ITS OWN

The question of how to structure a thesis and how to break it up into chapters is probably one of the most common. It's unlikely that you've had to write something made up of chapters before your thesis, and although it doesn't seem that difficult, actually finding the right structure for a thesis can be challenging.

How a thesis can be broken up into chapters varies by the type of thesis, the topic, and its academic discipline. Even two theses written on the same exact topic in the same discipline can be structured completely differently by their authors and the authors' preferences. We can't tell you specifically how to structure yours, but we can offer you a few guidelines.

Each chapter should encompass a complete idea or argument. For example, if you're working on an English thesis about a certain writer, perhaps each chapter can discuss a particular period in that writer's life and how it contributed and influenced the writer's works. Or maybe you're writing about two competing theories of economic development in a certain country. You can have a chapter about each of the theories and their backgrounds, and a few chapters that consider important economic events in the country through the two theoretical lenses. You get the point. Each chapter should contain a distinct and complete idea.

Another way to think about this is to imagine taking a chapter of your thesis and publishing it as a stand-alone paper or article. Does it present an idea and argue it? Does the reader feel like he or she is reading a completed piece of writing rather than a small piece of something larger?

You've succeeded halfway in structuring your thesis if each of your chapters presents a clear and complete idea and can stand confidently on its own.

> *"Think about your thesis chapters as a series of related papers. This will make your total page count less daunting as you start, and also keep you organized as you write."*
>
> **Political Science major,**
> **Princeton University '02**

A NOTE ON COUNTER-ARGUMENTS

As you formulate your thesis and its supporting arguments, remember that a strong argument isn't one that completely ignores or unabashedly rejects its opposing viewpoints. In fact, if you fail to present rival arguments and the rationale behind them, your thesis will appear biased and its persuasive powers will be weakened.

Your best bet is to become intimately familiar with all of the arguments that go against your own and argue clearly and logically why they're not appropriate or just plain wrong. Devote some time to stepping into the shoes of your rival thinkers and to figuring out why they believe what they do. This will help you write a more balanced thesis that persuades through its brilliant logic rather than through impassioned trampling of all opposing views.

DON'T WRITE A CHAPTER FOR A CHAPTER'S SAKE

The other half of the task of structuring your thesis is making sure that all of the chapters relate to and further the arguments in your thesis statement, and that they're all necessary to make it as strong as possible. You might be able to find a ton of fascinating material on a certain aspect of your topic and write a stellar chapter about it, but that won't make your thesis stronger if this particular aspect of your topic is not relevant to your overall argument. The chapter will be superfluous and will distract the reader. It will weaken your thesis and that's what you don't want to do.

A good mental test is to look at your thesis, taking a chapter at a time. Read your thesis argument and then look through the thesis with a particular chapter missing. You should feel like something is missing. You should feel that there is a hole in the argument, that there is not enough support for one of the assertions your thesis statement makes. Without that particular chapter, your thesis is not as strong as with it. Now you've got the validation for including that chapter in your thesis. Awesome.

As you think about your paper's structure, don't forget to use the short outline we talked about. It presents a quick picture of your thesis and you can use it to test whether there are unnecessary or missing chapters.

BE WILLING TO REWRITE

"You need to write in drafts. The first draft will always be terrible. Be prepared for several drafts to really convey your points."

**History major,
Wesleyan University '99**

You'll be much better off if you begin to write your thesis with the full expectation that much of what you write might eventually end up in the garbage—or in your computer's recycle bin. Tame your ambitions to get it right on the first try and don't stress out when you find that the last ten pages you've just written make absolutely no sense at all. If a good thesis could be written in just one draft, it's unlikely that colleges would allow us to have the whole year or semester to work on it.

Writing a great thesis and working through several drafts of each chapter requires a lot of guts, in addition to persistence and immense patience. Rewriting is different from editing. It is much more structural and fundamental. Only if you have guts will you be able to scrap a paragraph or a section because you think you can present your points better.

If you can find the guts to rewrite what can be made better, your thesis will have the best shot at being stellar. But, maybe more importantly, you'll have the best chance at feeling stellar for having done it, and for not having been lazy and careless. The worst feeling is to be walking back to your dorm after receiving your less-than-great thesis evaluation and feeling your mind get crowded with a bunch of "coulda shoulda"s.

THINK ABOUT YOUR READER

Yes, someone is actually going to read your thesis. It might be just a few people like your advisor and evaluators. Or, it might be many more if you're ambitious and persistent enough to get parts, or your entire thesis, published later on. But there will be a time when someone else's eyes other than your own will glide over the words, sentences, and paragraphs over which you've labored for many months.

Be aware of your reader as you write. Think about the degree of familiarity your intended reader might have with your subject. Figure out what might be worth explaining in more detail and what you can assume your reader already knows.

In general, it's safe to assume that your reader is an educated adult willing and ready to read academic literature. What you shouldn't assume is that your reader is fully versed in the specific terminology and concepts of your particular topic and academic discipline. Sure, it's likely that your future readers will either come from, or be interested in, the academic discipline in which your thesis belongs. But a historian should be able to read and understand your linguistics thesis, and a mathematician should not be confused by your sociology work.

Write clearly, explain esoteric words and concepts, and avoid using overly academic jargon. Each discipline has its jargon, and if you really must use it, then make sure to define your terms.

AVOID USING A STIFF AND FORMAL TONE

For some reason, when many of us begin to write a thesis we adopt a tone that is more formal and stiff than the one we usually use in our regular college papers. The thesis just seems more grand and formal, and we modify our tone accordingly. When we think of a thesis, we think of the many pieces of formal academic writing that we've read during college and the nauseatingly stiff tone in which many of those writings are presented.

Part of the reason for the formality of an academic piece of writing is valid—it's serious stuff written by a serious person. Part of it, however, is a way for academia to maintain its image of an exclusive, prestigious club. "If you can't read our books, then you aren't smart enough to be one of us."

Too highbrow for our taste. Your thesis should most definitely be smart and serious—even if you're writing on the subject of the history of comedy in Europe. (Creative writing theses are excluded from this sweeping generality, of course.) But your thesis shouldn't be dull and overly formal. As we just mentioned, someone is actually going to read your thesis. At a minimum, the reader should be able to get through most of it without taking more than two naps.

If you write in an extremely formal way, you make your thesis more difficult to read and less palatable for the reader. Instead, your goal is to draw the reader in. Think about this as you write and avoid using big words and formal, long-winded sentences just for the sake of making your thesis sound more "academic." Your thesis should sound like you talking about your topic in an intelligent and clear way.

DON'T OVERUSE EVIDENCE TO IMPRESS

Congrats if you've been able to find a ton of evidence to support your thesis and its central argument. That's an accomplishment all its own, so you should be proud. But try to avoid the temptation to include every great fact and figure.

By all means, you should definitely show off your amazing research skills and perseverance. There are many theses that suffer from poorly supported arguments and many thesis writers who don't go to enough lengths to find the necessary research to make their arguments stronger.

If you make an argument, you have to support it, and you should do so unabashedly.

What's not a great idea is to include supporting evidence for the sake of showing just how much of it you've found. The reader of your thesis should be persuaded and convinced by your fair and well-supported thesis argument. But not overwhelmed.

Impress with your logic, your ability to grasp and present complex issues in a clear and persuasive way, and with your inviting tone and breadth of knowledge. Leave the facts and figures to their proper role of supporting what you say.

GIVE CREDIT GENEROUSLY

While writing your thesis, you'll be drawing upon arguments, ideas, and thoughts that you've read during your research. Make sure that you clearly state when an idea you're presenting originated in someone else's mind or was presented in a particular publication. Give credit generously and wherever it belongs.

It's important to do this not just because you want to avoid any type of plagiarism. By indicating who is responsible for a particular point, you're letting the reader know that it is not you. You're also letting the reader be the judge of whether he/she wants to accept or reject the validity of that particular point based on who its author might be. That way, the reader is free to dismiss an argument because he or she feels a certain way towards the author, but can still read your thesis and your arguments without a strong bias.

A NOTE ON PLAGIARISM

Plagiarism is bad. You don't do yourself or anyone else any good if you copy things out of another source and present them under your own name. Even if you get a higher grade, your conscience will eat away at you. (Even if it doesn't at the time when you're plagiarizing.) Plagiarizing cheats you out of learning and feeling good about your work, and it cheats the author of the material you plagiarize out of proper recognition. Not to mention that if you get caught—and the chances are pretty high since professors tend to read and remember a ton of material—the consequences are beyond awful.

Even if you don't intend to plagiarize, be careful that you support your intentions with proper actions. Don't forget to mention sources when you're citing them. When you take notes while reading a source, indicate to yourself whether something you write is your idea or an idea from the source. You might inadvertently forget later on, and having a good record will help avoid problems.

Finally, just remember that you're smart and you don't need to borrow someone else's thoughts and ideas to write a great thesis.

MAKE YOUR CONCLUSION MORE THAN A SUMMARY

The core role of the conclusion to your thesis is to summarize the arguments and ideas you've presented, and to reaffirm your thesis statement (although avoid doing this verbatim). But a great conclusion is more than just a summary. In its finest form, it's a diving platform from which the reader can jump off into a much bigger and deeper set of thoughts and ideas that is related to your thesis.

At its base, the diving platform is stiff and firmly connected to the foundation of the pool. That's the beginning of your conclusion, the summary of what you've argued in your thesis, and the key arguments you've presented. But as you go out further onto the diving platform, it becomes more flexible. That's the middle of your conclusion. Here you can connect your thesis and its arguments to some broader issues you'd like the reader to consider. The tip of the diving platform has the greatest range of motion and the power to launch the diver into the air with confident force. That's the very end of your conclusion, the part where you should feel free to launch your reader's thoughts out of the bounds of your thesis and into the larger sphere of ideas and implications.

A powerful conclusion makes a difference. It's the last thing your reader will read, and we remember what we read first and last with more accuracy than what we read in the middle. Have some fun with it if you have the energy. It's your last hundred meters.

writing notes

_____

_____

_____

_____

_____

_____

_____

_____

_____

_____

_____

_____

_____

_____

_____

_____

revising and editing your thesis

If you follow our advice or your own judgment, you'll be rewriting your thesis drafts as you write them. In any case, you'll have to devote some time to carefully revising and editing your entire thesis once it's completed. However great your ideas and arguments might be, they won't come across as such unless your writing is easy to read and is free from various grammatical and spelling mishaps.

If you're reading this section because you've finished the first draft of your thesis, then stop before you do anything else. Stand up, take a deep breath, let it out, raise your hands in the air, spread your mouth into a smile, and loudly scream a few "yeahs" and "wows." Don't be bothered by the few strange looks you might get.

This might sound absurd, but try to enjoy the process of revising and editing your work. The hard parts are all over—the endless days of looking for that one book you must read, the late nights of staring at your computer screen, the hours of worry and frustration and just being really, really tired. You're almost done, and unless you've left yourself one day before the deadline to revise and edit your work, take the time to enjoy it. Grab a nice cup of the beverage of your choice, sit somewhere you like to be, and go through your thesis, page by page.

"What surprised me most about working on my thesis is the number of times that I ended up revising it."

**Russian Literature major,
Williams College '02**

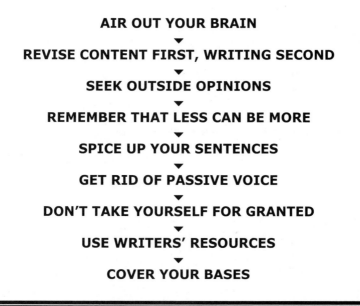

AIR OUT YOUR BRAIN
▼
REVISE CONTENT FIRST, WRITING SECOND
▼
SEEK OUTSIDE OPINIONS
▼
REMEMBER THAT LESS CAN BE MORE
▼
SPICE UP YOUR SENTENCES
▼
GET RID OF PASSIVE VOICE
▼
DON'T TAKE YOURSELF FOR GRANTED
▼
USE WRITERS' RESOURCES
▼
COVER YOUR BASES

AIR OUT YOUR BRAIN

If you have more than a few days to revise and edit your thesis before you have to turn it in, then take a break after you finish writing. Put away your computer, close the books, take out the earplugs, and get some space between your mind and your thesis. Both will very much appreciate it. And when you go back to begin the revisions, you'll be able to read your work with a much more independent and objective eye. And that's exactly what you need to really succeed at revising and editing.

REVISE CONTENT FIRST, WRITING SECOND

When you begin to revise your thesis, focus exclusively on its content, rather than on the writing. Try not to become too distracted by misspelled words, incomplete sentences, or misplaced paragraphs. Instead, focus on the clarity of the arguments, the consistency of your thesis statement with each chapter and each section, and the structure of your work.

Look for repetitive points or inadequately argued ideas. Ask yourself whether each argument is necessary and how you can improve it to strengthen your thesis and its overall clarity. Make sure that you can see and understand the flow of your thesis, and that it will make sense to someone not as intimately familiar with your topic.

Reading your thesis out loud to yourself as you revise it can be extremely helpful. You'll be more likely to notice inconsistencies and missing points, as well as hear repetitive sentences. Reading aloud will also help you hear your thesis in the way your readers will be hearing it from your words.

author's corner
▼
I spent a week carefully editing the grammar and style of my conclusion. Then I trashed it and rewrote it from scratch after it failed to work with the rest of the content changes I'd made in my thesis. A great waste of time, which I could have spent breathing fresh, spring air.
▲

SEEK OUTSIDE OPINIONS

To really do a great job revising your thesis, it is extremely helpful to get a few suggestions from people who are not you. One of these people is, of course, your advisor, who has been reading parts of your thesis as you worked on it, and, if possible, should read it once more when you've completed the first draft.

While your advisor's opinion is extremely valuable, he or she is not entirely objective and is too close to your thesis. If you can find another professor to read just a chapter or two and give you comments, absolutely grab that opportunity. In the ideal situation, this professor will not be more than slightly familiar with your thesis and might even teach in a different academic department. He or she will read your work with a cold, critical eye and you'll gain the most from the professor's comments. Because this is likely to take up a bit of the professor's time, be extremely polite and understanding when asking, and don't suggest that the professor read your entire work.

If your school has a writers' workshop or a similar resource, that's another great place to go for independent advice about your work. You probably won't be able to submit your entire thesis for review, so pick chapters that are either most critical or were most difficult for you to write. Remember that what you're after here is someone who is not too familiar with your topic. You might want to indicate that to the workshop members upfront.

To gain the most from having other people read your first draft, tell them upfront what type of feedback you're looking for and ask them a few targeted questions after they're done:

- What did they see as the central argument of your work?

- Which supporting points did they find stronger and what did they feel might have been missing?

- Was anything confusing?

- Can they make two or three suggestions of ways to improve your work?

Try to listen carefully and not dismiss their comments because they're not familiar with your topic. That's exactly the type of feedback that you want if you're interested in making your thesis strong and clear.

Don't forget to thank your readers a hundred times over. Perhaps you'll want to give them a copy of your completed thesis when you're all done.

> "Keep discussing your thesis with anyone who shows a mild interest in it. Some of the most illuminating comments I received came from unexpected sources."
>
> **Russian Literature major,**
> **Williams College '02**

REMEMBER THAT LESS CAN BE MORE

More words and sentences don't necessarily make a point stronger, and they can often make it more confusing. Comb through your thesis and get rid of unneeded stuff. It will become more succinct and read easier, and we doubt there are many schools that give higher praise for a higher page count.

SPICE UP YOUR SENTENCES

As writers we have writing habits. One of these is the way we tend to structure our sentences. Go through your thesis and make sure that your sentences are not all too similar or too long. Intersperse short and punchy sentences among the longer descriptions.

Varied sentence structure, especially in the same paragraph, makes your work more interesting to read. Just remember that each of your sentence's primary role is to communicate with the reader. Too much colorfulness may not be the best thing.

GET RID OF PASSIVE VOICE

No matter how many times we've heard our English teachers tell us to use the active voice instead of the passive, the latter still manages to somehow creep into our writing. While it's fine to have a few passive voice sentences here and there, your thesis will read much better if most of your sentences are active.

A quick refresher:

PASSIVE: "This subject was studied by several researchers."

ACTIVE: "Several researchers studied this subject."

DON'T TAKE YOURSELF FOR GRANTED

If you read something in your thesis that doesn't make much sense to you, try not to skip over it by thinking that it must have made sense when you wrote it. If something doesn't seem right, it probably isn't, and this is your chance to fix it. Reread the section to understand why it might be confusing. Is it the way it's written? Easy, rewrite it to make it clearer. Or, is the argument weaker than you thought? A bit more challenging, but if you just spend a few minutes thinking about it, you'll find a way to make it stronger.

The same goes for annotations, footnotes, and bibliographies. If you see something—such as a page number, source name, or author name—that doesn't seem to fit, take the two minutes needed to check it. Professors are picky about these seemingly minor details and you'd rather they focus on your writing, so make sure they don't become distracted.

USE WRITERS' RESOURCES

There are many great and helpful resources available to you as a writer while you work on your thesis. It's a good idea to remember them as you revise your work and to be willing to consult them if you need to. If you have general grammar or word usage questions, check out some of the popular writer's guides available at your college bookstore.

We've listed our favorites in the "**helpful resources**" section.

If your school has a writing workshop, take advantage of it. Writing tutors can help you improve the clarity of your writing, edit your work, and ensure that you're following fundamental formatting rules for your particular academic discipline.

If you want to go a step further and have another person edit your thesis, there are hundreds of freelance editors who can be easily found, locally or online. They charge quite a bit for their services, most often per page or per hour of their time. We don't necessarily recommend that you go this far. We trust that you're capable enough to tackle the editing of your work on your own, with help from a few reference books and your school's writers' workshop. But, if you feel that an outside editor is for you, you'll have no problem finding one. Just check a reference or two before you sign up, and make sure that your school's honor code doesn't prohibit it.

COVER YOUR BASES

Details count. Sometimes quite a bit.

- Check your grammar and check your capitalization.

- Check your spelling. The spell-check tool on your computer is a good first step. Focusing your own attentive eyes on your thesis pages is the necessary second.

- Find out the formatting requirements for your discipline and department and follow them.

- Make sure everything is spaced consistently and that you're using the same font throughout.

- Include page numbers and check that they're correct.

- Include a properly formatted Bibliography.

- Make sure that the page numbers are consistent with the Table of Contents.

- Make sure that you spell the name of your advisor and best friend correctly in the Acknowledgements.

revising and editing notes

_____

_____

_____

_____

_____

_____

_____

_____

_____

_____

_____

_____

_____

_____

the daily grind

Working on your thesis will be a grueling experience, however organized, brilliant, and prepared you might be. Here are a few ideas to help you keep your sanity.

▶FIND YOUR WORKING STYLE AND STICK WITH IT

Not everyone likes routines. Many of us, in fact, are free spirits for whom routines are unnecessary and limiting. But however you might generally feel about establishing routines in your life, it might make a lot of sense while you work on your thesis. A thesis is a special kind of project that requires a slightly more organized approach to get done well.

A routine doesn't have to mean anything more complicated than a general idea of how you will approach your days, weeks, and months as you work on your thesis. Are you going to try and work on some part of your thesis every day? Will you try and make some days thesis-free? Give this a bit of thought, and once you decide what will work best for you, stick with it. Knowing what you expect yourself to do with regard to your thesis on a daily basis will help you avoid getting frustrated and overwhelmed.

▶MAINTAIN PERSPECTIVE

A thesis is important, and because you're reading this guide, you're probably somewhat interested in doing a good job with it. Yes, grad schools like to see honors on your resume and yes, some colleges require an honors thesis to grant you those honors. Yes, your parents are on your back, and yes, in general you're a higher than average achiever.

But none of this is any reason to lose all common sense—together with sleep and human connections—while you work on your thesis. Maintain a degree of perspective, even on those long nights when you're stuck at the library and nothing else seems to be going on in life outside of your thesis carrel. A lot is, actually. You have friends, family, things you like to do, and other classes in which you're interested. Not to mention that most of us have to spend much of our senior year looking for a job or applying to graduate school. Those activities are just as important, and try not to forget that.

Don't let your thesis consume you. Immerse your mind in it, devote yourself to the process, and learn as much as you can from it. But don't lose your sanity by forgetting that your thesis is just one part of your life, however important and integral that part might be for much of your senior year.

▶BE YOUR OWN JUDGE

> "My advisor took me through twists and turns when I didn't need to twist or turn—but she was invaluable when the product was almost finished."
>
> **History major,**
> **University of Wisconsin '99**

Everyone works in a different way and at a different pace. Just because your roommate has already finished her fourth chapter when you're starting your second doesn't mean much beyond the fact that she has finished her fourth chapter and you're starting your second. Don't get caught up in what other people are doing. Focus on what you have to do instead.

Similarly, don't assume that your advisor knows all. Your advisor is not a robot, but a person with subjective opinions. If you disagree with one or more of them and you have a rational reason for doing so, then accept the fact that you disagree and follow your own instincts.

▶FIGHT FRUSTRATION WITH ACTION

Completing a thesis takes a long time and a lot of persistence. The probability that you'll get frustrated a few times during this period is pretty close to 100%. You can't find a certain source, or you can't figure out how to structure a chapter, or you just can't seem to write a single sentence that you like.

Don't let your frustration consume you. Fight it with concrete action. If you can't find a certain source, find one similar to it and use that one. If you can't structure a chapter, skip that part of your thesis and work on something else for a while. If you don't like what you're writing, try a free-writing exercise. Just type, without stopping or thinking about what your writing is like, and try to do this for five or ten minutes. Get your fingers and your brain out of the rut. You'll find that after a while you'll gain back your confidence.

And hey, don't be too shy or too proud to ask for help. Your advisor, writing workshop tutors, and your friends—they're all ready and willing. You just have to ask.

▶TAKE BREAKS

> *"Take up some scheduled physical activity. It will help with sleep problems, general health and sanity, and concentration."*

**College of Letters major,
Wesleyan University '01**

Breathe. Take breaks. Go for a walk. Read something completely unrelated to your thesis. Surf the Internet. Go running. Shoot pool. Paint.

Basically, try to get away from your thesis once in a while.

▶ALWAYS HAVE TWO OR MORE COPIES OF YOUR THESIS

This is huge. Make sure that you always, always, always have a backup copy of your thesis on both disk and paper. Always.

And don't forget to clearly label which version is from which date, so you don't spend two days revising an old version of chapter two.

▶ALLOW TIME TO HANDLE ADMIN TASKS

Unfortunately, writing, revising, and editing your thesis to perfection does not mean that you're all done and can freely enjoy the last few months of your senior year. Before you do that, you'll have to get your thesis printed, copied, and bound (if you so wish), turn it in for evaluation to the selected readers, and complete any paperwork your college or university might require. There are endless nightmarish stories of denied honors caused by missed deadlines and all sorts of other unpleasantries that you should avoid.

In order to avoid them, make sure that you know exactly what you have to do and by when. How many readers will be reading your thesis? How many copies do you need? When do you have to turn in your thesis and to whom? Do you have to deliver the copies to your readers personally? What is the best way to get the required number of copies of your thesis? (There is usually a printing place near campus that is used to dealing with stressed seniors and printing theses on time. Find this place well before you're ready to turn in your thesis and know exactly how long it takes to make the required number of copies).

No detail is too small or too silly. It all counts. Not only because you want to avoid negative consequences, but also because your nerves and peace of mind are important.

▶DON'T BINGE ON CAFFEINE

Coffee is every college student's friend. But it's a good idea to avoid over-caffeinating yourself as you work on your thesis. It can make you irritable and make it difficult to get the few hours of sleep for which you actually have time. Consume it in moderation, and substitute it often with fresh air or a crunchy snack, like an apple or a granola bar. It'll wake you up and help take out some frustration with that ridiculously useless source you just read.

what "they" say

We asked. They answered. Here are a few pieces of advice from professors and thesis advisors from Princeton, Georgetown, Swarthmore, and Brown. Since your professors might share a few of their opinions, it might be good to keep these in mind as you chart your own thesis course.

WHAT IS THE ONE PIECE OF ADVICE YOU'D GIVE TO THESIS WRITERS?

"Start early."

"Formulate an argument which you will elaborate in the thesis. Many students believe such an argument will arise, naturally, from their evidence. But that is seldom true."

"Accept your advisor's advice about what might be doable. It may not be precisely what you want to work on, but it is much more likely to be of lasting value."

HOW SHOULD STUDENTS APPROACH WORKING WITH THEIR ADVISOR?

"Find someone you feel comfortable with, regardless of their area of expertise, and then use them as much as possible."

"Don't be a stranger. Talk to your advisor as often as necessary and take their suggestions to heart."

"Meet the advisor early and insist on a schedule of meetings from that point on: make sure that you bind yourself to deliver portions of the thesis to the advisor during these later meetings."

WHAT DO YOU EXPECT FROM AN UNDERGRADUATE THESIS?

"Mostly that it be an exercise that teaches the undergraduate a set of new research skills. A concerted attempt to create something new is also critical."

"Hard work and a real effort to say something important and distinctive (even if the end product doesn't ultimately turn out that way). Good proofreading and editing also count."

"I expect a genuinely meditated and complex argument on an issue that matters to the writer. I expect a piece of prose that has managed to take on weight, complexity, and balance."

helpful resources

Below are a few of our favorite resources to help you as you work on your thesis.

But before you reach for a book or access a website, make sure you're taking advantage of the resources offered by your school. Many offer writing workshops, thesis templates and formatting guides, workshops on research techniques, and many other immensely helpful tools. Your school's resources are free and you don't have to go looking for them. Don't neglect them.

BOOKS

The Elements of Style, by William Strunk, Jr., E.B. White, Charles Osgood, and Roger Angell. Allyn & Bacon, 4th Edition, 2000.

Chances are you haven't gotten through college without this succinct, well-written, and extremely useful book that covers the basics of grammar and writing style. If it's escaped your bookshelf, you might want to spend a few dollars and use this great resource as you begin to write, and when you revise and edit.

MLA Handbook for Writers of Research Papers, by Joseph Gibaldi. Modern Language Association of America, 5th edition, June 1999.

A very popular—for good reasons—and very useful resource to help you through the researching and writing process. It includes sections on research, narrowing your topic, taking notes, evaluating authors, and formatting your writing, footnotes, and bibliographies. Offers some helpful ways to cite electronic sources. This book is somewhat of a bible in academia. Buy it, use it, keep it on your shelf, and feel like a true academic.

The next few books on our list come from the University of Chicago Press. No, we are not getting paid for including them on our guide. But yes, after scouring the bookstores for useful, intelligent, and non-gimmicky resources, we found that the University of Chicago Press had a kind of monopoly on the market. Here are a few we particularly like:

Manual for Writers of Term Papers, Theses, and Dissertations, by Kate L. Turabian. University of Chicago Press, 6th Edition, 1996.

This is a less technical and overwhelming alternative to the *Manual of Style* and a straightforward and very useful resource. Some of the best sections are *Components of a Paper, Bibliographies,* and *Sample Layouts.*

The Chicago Manual of Style: The Essential Guide for Writers, Editors, and Publishers, by John Grossman (Preface). University of Chicago Press, 14th Edition, 1993.

All the possible formats and requirements made it in, and although it's extremely technical, if you use it rather than read it, you'll impress your readers (and graders) with proper academic formatting. Believe us, it counts.

The Craft of Research, by Wayne C. Booth, Gregory G. Colomb, and Joseph M. Williams. University of Chicago Press, 1995.

If you're really serious about doing a great job with your research and not keeling over in the process, use this book. It is filled with suggestions—albeit, written in a very didactic academic style—about structuring your analyses and arguments, using questions and introductions to guide your research, and avoiding common pitfalls. One of the book's greatest qualities is the way it ties research to the overall goal of writing a term paper or a thesis—that is, to present a cohesive, well-researched, and solidly expressed argument.

If you're working on a psychology thesis, here's a resource you probably won't be able to escape:

Publication Manual of the American Psychological Association, July 2001.

A super-technical guide on how to appropriately format your thesis according to APA guidelines. Take it out from the library and use it sparingly.

WEBSITES

www.questia.com

Someone felt the pain of thousands of thesis writers searching through library shelves at two in the morning and created Questia, the largest online library where—with an Internet connection and a few dollars per month—you can read through thousands of social science and humanities books, make notes, create footnotes and bibliographies, and never lose track of a single page. Start with a trial membership to check it out.

www.thesaurus.com

An easy-to-use online version of the ever-necessary Roget's Thesaurus. You can search for synonyms by word or topic, just like in the book version. So, if you don't feel like flipping pages, this is a great tool.

www.dictionary.com

You got it—it's an online dictionary. It's easy to use and always there to help you.

STRESS RELIEVERS

Post It® Flags

These little stickers will save your life. Buy a bunch and use them to mark pages and paragraphs. If you're really organized, you can color coordinate by chapter, but no need to get crazy about it.

www.theonion.com

This is an absolutely fun and hilarious website that can provide hours upon hours of wonderfully refreshing stress relief. Use it. It will help.

Granola bars

They're crunchy. They're filling. They're great frustration absorbers.

the final word

"Curiously, the most rewarding thing about working on a thesis was the very process of expending massive quantities of energy on a very small problem."

**History major,
Wesleyan University '99**

Seems like regardless of schools and majors, theses always turn out both more and less of what we expected. More challenging, more rewarding, and taxing of more of our skills than just reading and writing. Less intimidating, less boring, and perhaps less life-important in retrospect.

When it's all done and a copy of your magnus opus sits on your desk, your parents' bookshelf, or your advisor's bookshelf, don't forget to appreciate the huge undertaking you've just accomplished. At the risk of sounding like a Hallmark card, researching and writing an undergraduate thesis is a big deal and you should feel pretty great about yourself for taking on the task. As a bonus, you've probably learned a few things in the process, whether it was about an academic discipline or about yourself.

And that's never a bad thing.

"After all the ups and downs of college, I feel that I finished on a high note with my thesis, completing what only a few years before seemed impossible— writing one hundred pages of my very own."

**Theater and Psychology major,
Hampshire College '02**